LEADERS GUIDE
TRUTH
— AND —
LOGIC
FOR YOUR TEEN

Giving Our Teens a Solid Foundation of Truth

DAVI BURKE

WESTBOW
PRESS®
A DIVISION OF THOMAS NELSON
& ZONDERVAN

WestBow Press books may be ordered through booksellers or by contacting:

WestBow Press
A Division of Thomas Nelson & Zondervan
1663 Liberty Drive
Bloomington, IN 47403
www.westbowpress.com
1 (866) 928-1240

ISBN: 978-1-5127-9100-6 (sc)
ISBN: 978-1-5127-9101-3 (e)

Print information available on the last page.

WestBow Press rev. date: 11/17/2017

Contents

Chapter 1

THE BEGINNING

As you are growing up and making decisions, both for the present and future, you could be wondering what will happen next. There is a God who is interested in you and desires to be involved in all you do. He is a God that loves you. He is your Creator. He knew you from the very beginning.

There are a lot of people out there that insist God does not exist. They insist that everything and anything is acceptable. These views will lead you to decisions that bring sadness and emptiness as you grow up. Some turn to drugs, some to alcohol. Others gambling or a variety of other things to fill that emptiness. There are instructions that are right. If you trust these instructions you will find a true and meaningful happiness.

Let's look at the basic commandments that God gave us in the Old Testament. Today we live under God's grace thanks to Jesus. We will learn about that in a later chapter, but these are still very good guidelines that help us to have a great life. We will look at each one to better understand why God gave His people these instructions to follow.

God gave us the Ten Commandments to establish guidelines and boundaries in order for society to function in harmony. The first four commandments establish mans relationship with God. The last six commandments establish mans relationship with man. These commandments were written literally by the finger of God. Isn't that amazing!

Read Exodus 31:18

*And when God had made an end of speaking with Moses on Mount Sinai, He gave Moses two tablets of the Testimony (Commandments) on tablets of stone, **written with the finger of God.** Isn't that incredible!*

Read Exodus 20: 1-17

1.) *I am the Lord your God. You shall have no other god's before Me.*

Exodus 20:2,3

What does this mean?

> God reminds us that He is our Lord. Let's look at the title 'Lord' for a minute. Lord means one having power and authority over others. Having ownership or possession through inheritance. A hereditary right to whom service and obedience are due.

> God identifies Himself as the Great King of the universe. He is perfect in power, wisdom and kindness. We are His creation. We are not to elevate any false idea or thing that takes away our worship from Him and place it on a powerless elevated idea or concept .

Why do you think this is important to God?

> He knows that when we look to other things or ideas as 'gods', they are powerless and useless. The consequences are devastating. It opens the door to other evils bringing unbelief towards Him. It limits our view of who He is and what He can do. He knows it will ultimately limit His power and blessings in our life.

Was this commandment made for God or us? Why?

> The commandment was made for us.

> God is warning us that if we look to futile gods, we will separate ourselves from Him, our true helper and savior. He alone is to be worshiped, obeyed and adored.

2.) *You shall not make for yourself any idols. For I, the Lord your God, am a jealous God.* **Exodus 20:4,5**

What does this mean?

An idol is a false god. An object of extreme devotion. It is any thing or image that is substituted for God in your heart. Think about that. If you take the time to worship an idol, you are placing your hope and expectations on a man made thing instead of the living God. Worship is placing extravagant respect or admiration for an object of worth or of high regard.

Can you think of one? How about money, sports or maybe even your cell phone.

Why would God get jealous?

First, lets look at what jealousy means. It is intolerant of rivalry or unfaithfulness. Also, it is vigilant or watchful and alert in guarding a possession. Doesn't that make sense. God's great love for us protects our relationship with him as a valuable possession. Thus, Gods jealousy is a righteous jealousy, because He knows what will happen to us if we worship other things. He wants us! I hope that makes you feel special. Because you are! It certainly makes me feel special.

3.) *You shall not take the name of the Lord your God in vain.*

Exodus 20:7

What does this mean?

The meaning of the word 'vain' is to have no real value or marked by ineffectiveness. When the Lord's name is used in vain, it is trivializing Him and His name by regarding it as insignificant.

Can you see why God commands us not to take His name in vain? God's name is holy, just as He is holy. God is our source of value. He is the great I AM. He is our Protector. He is our Provider. He is our Savior. He is our Redeemer. When we use His name in vain, we are inappropriately reducing Him to our level.

4.) *Remember the Sabbath day. To keep it holy.*

Exodus 20:8

What does this mean?

Let's read Genesis 2:1-3

Thus, the heavens and the earth, and all the host of them, were finished. And on the seventh day God ended His work which He had done, and He rested on the seventh day from all His work which He had done. Then God blessed the seventh day and sanctified it, because in it He rested from all His work which God had created and made.

God created the heavens and the earth and everything in it in six days. On the seventh day He rested, wherefore the Lord blessed the sabbath day or seventh day, and made it holy. God made the work week while creation was taking place. On each day of creation, He declared that the evening came and it completed that day. This is to confirm a day is twenty four hours and not thousands or millions of years. Never depart from the scriptures regardless of what others say. God chose creation in a literal six days. When His work was completed, He made the day of His completion holy. He didn't rest out of exhaustion but with a great joy of achievement. Man's rest on this day is not just an act of communion with God, but a thankful reflection of that event in which God Almighty gave a noble origin to the human race.

Look at the day, week, month and year. The week is the only time frame that has no astrological ties. The day is a period of an average length of time for the earth to make one rotation on its axis. In contrast, the week is a time frame for man. The month is a period of one complete revolution for the moon to travel around the earth. A year consists of one revolution for the earth to travel around the sun.

5.) *Honor your father and your mother that your life may be long upon the land which the Lord your God is giving you.*

Exodus 20:12

What does this mean?

This is the first commandment with a promise. God designed the parent-child relationship as one of mans most vital relationships. Honor means to respect or hold in high regard with integrity. We need to value and respect our parents. If you honor your parents, you will honor others. The things that your parents say and do that bless you, do to others. Pray for them when they do not meet your expectations. That is hard, but rewarding.

Does anyone want to pray for your parents or for the strength to carry this commandment out? God knows that your parents aren't perfect. Team up with someone that can give you good advice when you struggle with your parent relationship. You will be blessed.

When we honor God, we have a promise of protection, guidance, deliverance and provision. If we honor our parents, we will have a fulfilling well lived life.

6.) *You shall not murder.*

Exodus 20:13

Explain: Why?

Because we are made in the image of God. (Genesis 9:6) The shedding of innocent blood is disrespect toward God Himself.

In some Bibles, you will see this commandment with the word murder and in others you will see the word kill. Either way, it is referring to killing or murdering outside of the law. An unlawful murder puts guilt on the person that committed the crime or injustice. Think about it. If someone lawlessly kills another person, isn't that the complete opposite of what God requires from us, to love our neighbors as ourselves. The action is extreme destruction. It is evil in it's fullest state.

There are three situations where killing is not considered murder. In warfare, capital punishment and self defense. If another country calls for war against us and we had to fight to survive, we would be innocent of anyone we would have to kill to protect ourselves. If someone kills an innocent person, it is lawful to put him to death. If someone broke into your home and you killed the person while protecting yourself, you would be innocent in God's eyes.

7.) *You shall not commit adultery.*

Exodus 20:14

What does this mean?

Adultery is sexual relations between a married person and someone other than his or her lawful spouse. The marriage is a symbol of faithfulness. A union made by God. It is steadfast in affection and loyalty. It is firm in commitments and promises. It is a strong assurance.

Can you see what adultery could do to the people in a marriage? It can destroy everything that God binds together. When I think of all the qualities that a good marriage possesses, I think of security. If adultery enters, I see broken loyalty, weak assurance, unfaithfulness, broken promises, and broken commitments. The lack of security will lead to a broken heart and broken people.

Can you see why God said not to?

8.) *You shall not steal.*

Exodus 20:15

Explain: Why?

What is stealing? It is taking something from someone without the right or without detection. That makes it wrong. To take a possession with no regard to the person who rightfully owns it. If you had permission, you could do so in accordance with what is right and proper in conduct.

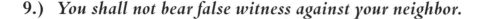

9.) *You shall not bear false witness against your neighbor.*

Exodus 20:16

What does this mean?

>   **Producing a false testimony or accusations to cause someone undue harm is the opposite of what God says. We should love our neighbors as ourselves.**

10.) *You shall not covet your neighbors house, wife or anything he owns.*

Exodus 20:17

What does this mean?

>   **God is warning us not to have strong envious desires toward someone else or what someone else owns, that is not available to us. This commandment is dealing with our minds. It is warning us to turn away from evil thoughts or wrongful desires that could lead to action if we don't protect ourselves.**

You have probably heard that these commandments are old or outdated.

Some say that they were ok for the people back then, but we are more modern now and have moved past these instructions.

If the same God created us from the beginning until now, why would He change His right living with time? Why would time change what is right?

Time makes people change, not God.

As people compromise, it is easier to accept what is wrong as acceptable. Not with God, because He doesn't accept what is wrong or any compromise to His holiness. Open your heart as we go through these different chapters to hear about God and that He really exists, and since He does, who He is!

Always start your time with prayer. Be specific to the area of your studies. Ask the Holy Spirit to open the hearts and minds of our youth with understanding and hope as they investigate into the personal God of the universe! Amen!

Who do you think God is?

We know who God is right! Our Creator, our Healer, our Savior, our Protector, our Father, our Comforter. We can go on and on with His attributes.

Give the teenagers a chance to really think about this question and write an answer. Ask them to be honest and sincere. Encourage them to take this time to write down what they really believe. Or maybe what they don't believe. The best answer is honesty without fear of what others think. Pray for the Holy Spirit's guidance. The goal here is to see where each teen is so you can specifically pray and ask God to work in those areas.

After they have completed this question, let them share without interruption, (unless they need help bringing their thoughts to an end). You can set a timer for each person sharing if you find they want to give long answers that take away from your goal.

What made you come to this conclusion?

Again, encourage honesty and truth. Their errors are what we can help them with. In the same manner give them time to think about the question and write about it. Each teen has his or her own conclusion depending on what they have learned or experienced. Let each share their answer. This is great insight into our youth.

Does your conclusion line up with a foundation of truth?

> **Their conclusion will be based on a variety of factors. These factors can include what they've heard, read, seen on tv, or even learned in school.**
>
> **Truth is being in accord with facts or reality.**
>
> **If their conclusion is not based upon the solid foundation of Jesus, then it will be faulty. This will give you insight into each teens understanding and will better help you to guide each individual to the truth.**

How?

> **Or maybe even why? This is where you can better understand the reasoning behind what they currently believe.**

What questions or doubts do you have?

> **This is open discussion time on what has been covered to this point. For the teen to ask questions or share doubts is what you want from them. After the questions have been answered and the doubts shared, have him or her write their own question or doubt down along with a solid answer for them to reflect on.**

Can you summarize the ten commandments in your own words and what they mean to you?

> **Give them time to write their thoughts. Let them share.**

Chapter 2

PROOF THAT GOD EXISTS

To understand the proof, you need to look at the facts to determine what is true and valid.

Let's use a sugar cookie as an example. We usually see these cookies after they are made and recognize them as sugar cookies but we really don't think any more about it. In reality, they come from somewhere. They do not start out as a cookie. They have a beginning. When you examine them, you find that they have these basic ingredients: flour, sugar and eggs.

The flour, sugar and eggs also have a beginning. Flour comes from wheat, sugar comes from the sugar cane and eggs come from the chicken. If we look into it further, we can still break some of these things down even more. The wheat and sugar cane both come from a seed. Because we cannot break the seeds or the chicken down any further, we can conclude based on the facts, where the sugar cookie comes from.

Where does the seed and the chicken come from?

Read Genesis 1:1-27. It starts with '*In the beginning....*'

The fact is, there is a beginning or starting point where *everything* comes from. That beginning or starting point is the place where it cannot be reduced or broken down any further.

When it comes to determining truth, the starting point is logic.

What is logic?

Logic is the foundation or base of the process when examining or searching for truth.

Logic is the correct thinking that leads to valid conclusions. It allows you to evaluate truths and reasoning for consistency and coherence or interconnection. In other words, a valid conclusion will flow in harmony with truth and reasoning. It will make sense.

What does this mean to you?

Let's look at the sugar cookie again. It is easy to look at a sugar cookie and say, yes, this is a sugar cookie. Why? Because during your life, someone gave you a cookie and said, 'this is a sugar cookie'. You trusted the source and therefore, believed it to be a sugar cookie. If you questioned the matter, you would need to take the sugar cookie and examine it's contents. You would research sugar cookies, to find out what they consist of, so you can make a logical conclusion based on your findings.

There is nothing before the first principles of logic. Logic can not be broken down further. So if logic proves something then it can't be disproved.

Why? Because logic is the foundation of right and correct thinking.

Do you understand what logic does? Is the example of the sugar cookie logical?

Give them time to write and think this through.

Can you give your own example of logic?

Have some fun with this. Ahead of time, come up with your own example. Think of something that will help simplify what you are trying to say. Have the group as a team come up with their own.

A first principle of logic is a basic foundation of truth that supports itself. The most important first principle of logic is the law of non-contradiction. In other words, the law of non-contradiction verifies logic which leads to truth.

What is non-contradiction?

The definition is that two opposite things can not be true at the same time, in the same sense. For example, there is cereal in the cupboard or there is not cereal in the cupboard. They both can not be true at the same time. In just the same way, either God exists or He does not exist? They both can not be true. The simple law of non-contradiction gives us a glimpse into the brilliance of God.

How?

Give your teens time to write an answer. Let someone read the answer from the book.

Because any attempt to deny the law of non-contradiction ends up validating it. In other words, the law of non-contradiction is proven by saying its not true.

If you say that the law of non-contradiction is not always true, then you are saying that contradictions can both be true at the same time. What is contradiction? A statement that implies both the truth and falsity of something. For example, a round square.

Both parts of a contradiction cannot possibly be true at the same time.

Take a minute to think about what was just read. Can you write in your own words what this means?

Let your teens answer this question as a group.

Can you give an example?

Let the teens take time as a group to come up with their own example. If the youth are struggling, you can coach them with your example so they can work it through as a team. Here are a few examples.

- ★ **The lights are on in the room and the same lights are not on in the room.**

- ★ **It is daytime here and it is night time here.**

- ★ **We have a beginning and we always existed.**

In each of these examples, both statements can not be true at the same time.

Let's give another example. Two opposites can not be true at the same time. The opposite of that is that two opposites can be true at the same time. But are both of those true? No. So by denying the law of non-contradiction, we end up proving it. The point is to show that logic is the bottom line. Nothing can undo what logic and what it's first principle non-contradiction can prove..

Does this make sense to you? Explain.

Give the teens time to respond. Encourage them to write down their thoughts. Logic, and the law of non-contradiction are so important for our youth to understand. If they do not understand this foundation, then others can come into their lives later on and fool them into unbelief.

Satan fools smart people, and uses them to fool other people. More often than not, logical fallacies, or deceptions are what is used to trip people up. There are dozens of these fallacies. A logical fallacy is saying something that sounds right, but if you stopped and really looked at the content, the meaning is something different.

Let's look at a couple.

The first one will be a person focusing on his friend in a statement instead of looking at the issue.

If one friend said to another, "Why do I need Jesus? You do wrong things too!"

Do you see the fallacy or deception in this?

Give the teens time to write down their thoughts.

There are two different issues here.

What are they?

Give the teens time to write down their thoughts.

The person speaking needs Jesus, and the second persons sinful nature is obvious.

Is his salvation dependent on the actions of his friend? No. So his statement is changing the focus from the fact that he needs Jesus to his friends actions.

Can you explain?

Give the teens time to write down their thoughts. If the teen does not understand what the fallacy is in this scenario, they would most likely stumble over their sin and the focus would shift away from the friend needing Jesus.

This one will focus on a statement at school.

While in class you read that people evolved from apes or fish and the teacher validates it as truth.

Does that make it true? No.

The statement is relying on the writer or the speaker. If the writer doesn't have the facts right, then your getting false information.

Have you heard this before? Explain.

Give the teens time to write down their thoughts.

Remember, the ape and fish had to have had a beginning!! If you are told they evolved, they still had to have had a beginning!! Fallacies, when investigating them, fall apart.

Can you give an example of a logical fallacy or deception?

Let us look back at the sugar cookie. What if someone had told you that it was a chocolate cookie before you ever did the research, your research would prove that it was a sugar cookie. You would realize that you were not given the correct information. You would have been told a fallacy.

Another example of a logical fallacy or deception is found in the statement that all religions are true. They all have different belief systems that point in different directions.

Some believe you have to earn your way to heaven by being good enough. Some do not believe there is a heaven at all. Some believe that whatever is true for you is true. On and on it goes. However, if you were to look at each one, they all contradict each other. How can they all be true? In the end, there is only one right answer. One God and One Way. But to prove this, you must look at the evidence.

Give an example of what others have shared with you?

Give the teens time to answer. Encourage each teen to write what they have encountered.

Does it line up with truth? Why or why not?

Encourage each one to write what he or she has encountered. Ask them to share. Is anyone being pressured into a belief that just does not line up with the truth? Ask if he or she is able to compare what is being said with what the Bible says.

The greatest question of all time is, 'why is there something instead of nothing?' Nothing can't create something. If something now exists, something always had to exist.

Not only do we exist, but we exist in a universe. So, either the universe always existed or something outside the universe always existed.

What does this mean to you?

Nothing can not create something. To be able to create something, something has to already exist.

For nothing to create something, it must both exist and not exist at the same time. This is a logical contradiction. Why? Because if it

is nothing, it does not exist. But to create something it would have to exist.

Creator (something) = creation

Nothing (nothing) = nothing

Nothing = something = a contradiction

What does the universe consist of? It consist of time, space and matter.

Can you find where time, space and matter are in the Bible?

Give a moment for the teens to think about what is being asked. Let them share what they have concluded.

Read Genesis 1:1

In the beginning (time), God created the heavens (space), and the earth (matter).

There are at least five proofs that men, some not believing in God, have discovered that the universe had a beginning.★ (Read the five proofs in the back of the book.) That means that time, space and matter had a beginning just as the Bible states.

Albert Einstein discovered that time, space and matter not only had a beginning but they all came into existence at the same time. Since they came into existence, they had a beginning. If something has a beginning, then it has a beginner. The beginner of time, space and matter has to be outside of the universe.

So the creator of time, space and matter has to be timeless, spaceless, and immaterial. In addition, the creator has to be personal because He chose to create. Also, the creator has to be intelligent because we have intelligence and you cannot give what you do not have. Further, the creator has to be powerful because He created the universe and is the source of all power in the universe.

Thus, the Beginner of the universe has to be timeless, spaceless, immaterial, powerful, personal and intelligent. Isn't this the basic definition of God?

Talk this through. The understanding behind this is very significant.

Therefore, it is not surprising that our universe is finely tuned for life to exist. One example, is found in our air, which is 21% oxygen. If it were higher, for instance 35%, everything on the earth would burn up. If it were lower, around 16% we would all suffocate. But, it's not just the air, it's gravity, temperature, the earth aligning with the sun and moon, etc.... think about that! There are actually more than one hundred and twenty different variables in all, that are just as precisely tuned for life. Many scientists now believe that the universe was fine tuned just so that we could exist. If even one of these variables were changed ever so slightly, there would be no life at all.

How amazing is that!

Can you explain in your own words what this means to you?

Give the teens time to write and talk about what it means to them.

Here are a couple examples:

1) Oxygen

Even though oxygen is in the air that we breath and is vital for us to exist, oxygen is a type of gas. This is why we are told not to light a match around oxygen tanks. Oxygen by itself is not explosive, but a spark next to it can ignite an explosion. The higher the percentage of oxygen, the more sensitive it is to a spark or flame. Fire needs oxygen to burn. If there were no oxygen, not only could nothing burn but we would suffocate, life could not exist. In contrast, at 25% oxygen, the things around us will catch fire much easier. At around 30% oxygen, it will take very little for fires to ignite. Fires would be popping up all around us.

2) Gravity

Gravity is the force that keeps us on the earth. However, it is not so strong as to crush us and not so weak that we would float off into space. Under either one of these scenarios, we could not survive if the gravitational force was not as precise as it is.

3) Temperature

Look at the temperature of the planet. Can you imagine if the temperature fluctuated between 200 degrees fahrenheit and -150 degrees below zero. We could not exist.

4) Distance Earth and Moon

If the earth were closer or farther from the moon the gravitational pull would change. The oceans tides would be very different. This would cause tidal waves and other crazy weather patterns.

Can you see the point. All these things are not an accident. Something intelligent had to put all of these variables into place at just the precise amount for us to exist. Isn't this amazing!

Even though God is the creator of the universe, and everything in it, He is intimate and personal.

Read 1 Kings 18:21

And Elijah came to the people and said, "How long will you falter between two opinions? If the Lord is God, then follow Him....."

Chapter 3

WHY THE BIBLE

Now that I see God as the Creator, why is the Bible the book that I should read?

First, let us understand why we go to the Bible for answers. The Bible isn't just a book. The Bible was inspired by God through His Holy Spirit. There are sixty six books in the Bible. Thirty nine books were written before Jesus came and twenty seven books written after He came. They were written by 40 chosen men over about a 1500 year time frame. These men came from all different backgrounds. Some were written by kings, military leaders, peasants, philosophers, fishermen, tax collectors, poets, musicians and statesmen.

He chose these men to be His voice through His word. They wrote the Bible in close prayer and obedience to Gods instruction.

Read 2 Timothy 3:16

All Scripture is given by inspiration of God, and is profitable for doctrine, for reproof, for correction, for instruction in righteousness that the man of God may be complete, thoroughly equipped for every good work.

Isn't that incredible! The Bible will give us every answer we need to have a life full of good work. He wants us to 'get it'! To have this 'life of good work', we cannot compromise His holiness with opinions that contradict His word. This is where you really need to put logic into practice. Use logic to find the truth. When a statement is being made that doesn't sound right. Think about the motive behind what is being said. Can you line up the statement with what God's word says?

Can you tell me in your own words what this means to you?

This example is in Scripture. God gave us His word so that we are equipped for every good work. What is the good work? What are the talents God gave you? If it is singing, and you are trusting God with your voice, you will be blessed to sing His praises for others to enjoy and be blessed. When we fully trust and believe His word He will use us for His glory. How exciting is that!

Can you give an example?

Leaders, ask each teen what they are good at. Explain that those things they are good at are gifts that God gave to them at birth just so they can have something to use when they want to serve God. Take the gift that they share with the group and explain how it can be used to serve God.

Now, let us look at some of the ways that God has revealed Himself in His word. This is where God has made Himself very evident.

In the Bible, there are 31,124 verses. Out of these verses, the Old Testament has approximately 1,239 scriptures that contain prophecy and the New Testament has approximately 578. Thats a total of 1,817 predictions. That means that approximately 26.8% of the Bible involves prophecy or in other words, the prediction of what is to come.

Within all of these books that the chosen men wrote with the instruction from God, there are hundreds of prophecies written about the coming of Jesus, why He was coming, and that He would die for us. The prophecies were also written to prepare us for what is to come in this world so that we wouldn't be surprised at the things happening around us today. These prophecies have been 100% true so far, by happening exactly how the Bible claimed they would, and within those prophecies, 75% have been fulfilled. Fulfilling prophecy is one proof that the Bible is Gods word. No religious book can compare to it in prophetic terms.

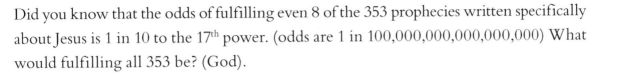

Did you know that the odds of fulfilling even 8 of the 353 prophecies written specifically about Jesus is 1 in 10 to the 17th power. (odds are 1 in 100,000,000,000,000,000) What would fulfilling all 353 be? (God).

Do you think prophecy is important in the Bible?

Yes!

Why or why not?

Because no other book can compare to it in prophetic terms. Only someone outside of time can know the future. Throughout the Bible, it has explained how this world began and how it will end. So far the Bibles prophecies have been 100% correct.

In the times of Jesus, many of the people that witnessed what He was doing wrote about Him. Even when some did not want to believe in Him as the Savior of the world, they still wrote about the great things He did. People were awed at His miracles! There is no doubt that Jesus lived and did what the Bible claims He did!

When we look in the land (Israel), where Jesus walked and lived, there is evidence of His existence. They have found many sights where He walked and preached to the world about who He is and why He came.

So far, there have been more than 25,000 archeological finds, or in other words, artifacts, inscriptions, monuments and other such remains, that verify facts in the Bible. Not one has been discovered to disprove it. Daily they are excavating and finding more.

The last place we will look into God's word to see His foreknowledge is involving science. The Bible is not a scientific text book. Despite this, it lists scientific discoveries thousands of years before scientists discovered them.

For example: Psalms 19:6 Gods spokesman wrote that the sun follows a circular path through the universe. This was written 3000 years ago.

In 700 BC, Isaiah 40:22 and Psalm 103:12 Gods spokesman writes that the earth is a circle.

Around 4000+ years ago Job 26:7 Gods spokesman wrote that the earth is suspended over nothing, and writes about the rain cycle over the earth.

How important is the scientific discoveries that were proven after the Bible was written? *In other words, scientific discoveries that have been discovered were written in the Bible long before the discoveries.*

It validates what we have been saying! God told us through the Bible about these facts, centuries before man discovered them.

Do they help validate the authority of Gods word?

Yes!

Why or why not?

As we discussed earlier, facts will flow in harmony with truth, logic and the law of non-contradiction. It validates what is true and valid.

Does anyone have any questions or doubts that you would like to talk about?

Take a few minutes and write down what has had an impact on you.

We have looked at prophecy, archeology, and science. These as I said earlier are just a few. All of creation has God's hand print all over it. We have no excuse to deny His existence.

Read Philippians 2:5-11

> *Let this mind be in you which was also in Christ Jesus, who, being in the form of God, did not consider it robbery to be equal with God, but made Himself of no reputation, taking the form of a bondservant, and coming in the likeness of men. And being found in appearance as a man, He humbled Himself and became obedient to the point of death, even the death of the cross. Therefore God also has highly exalted Him and given Him the name which is above every name, that at the name of Jesus every knee shall bow, of those in heaven, and of those on earth, and that every tongue shall confess that Jesus Christ is Lord, to the glory of God the Father.*

We will all bow our knees to Jesus. Whether we have accepted Him as our Lord and Savior or not. We will all see His glory and bow. Some going to heaven and some not.

Where will you be? If you are unsure about your answer, lets talk about it. There could be one thing you don't understand and have chosen to put your eternal destiny in jeopardy.

Chapter 4

LET'S LOOK AT WHO JESUS IS

Jesus was and has always been with God. He came to earth for us.

Read John 1:1,2

> *In the beginning was the Word, and the Word was with God, and the Word was God. He (Jesus) was in the beginning with God.*

How did He come to earth? What makes Him different than any other person being born?

Give the youth time to answer.

He couldn't be born from both a human mother and father because He would have been a sinner like us. He did have a human mother that gave birth to Him. However, He didn't have a human father. It was the Holy Spirit who came upon Mary and the power of the most high over shadowed her. Mary conceived a child with this great miracle. This is the God part of who Jesus is. He was 100% human and 100% God. This is where He gets his name, 'The Son of God.'

Read Luke 1:26-35

Now in the sixth month the angel Gabriel was sent by God to a city of Galilee named Nazareth, to a virgin betrothed to a man whose name was Joseph, of the house of David. The virgin's name was Mary. And having come in, the angel said to her, "Rejoice, highly favored one, the Lord is with you; blessed are you among women!" But when she saw him, she was troubled at his saying, and considered what manner of greeting this was. Then the angel said to her, "Do not be afraid, Mary, for you have found favor with God And behold, you will conceive in your womb and bring forth a Son, and shall call His name Jesus. He will be great, and will be called the Son of the highest; and the Lord God will give Him the throne of His father David. And He will reign over the house of Jacob forever, and of His kingdom there will be no end."

Then Mary said to the angel, "How can this be, since I do not know a man?"

And the angel answered and said to her, "The Holy Spirit will come upon you, and the power of the Highest will overshadow you; therefore, also, that Holy One who is to be born will be called the Son of God.

Take some time at home and read the first four books of the New Testament.

These books are Matthew, Mark, Luke and John. You will read all about Jesus and how powerful He is. At the same time, you will see Him very humble and His concern for the people around Him by the miracles of healing that He did. In the pages you will see Jesus' same love and concern for you. When He willingly went to the cross and was crucified, that was His ultimate sacrifice of love to you.

Read Matthew 28:1-8

Now after the Sabbath, as the first day of the week began to dawn, Mary Magdalene and the other Mary came to see the tomb. And behold, there was a great earthquake; for an angel of the Lord descended from heaven, and came and rolled back the stone from the door, and sat on it. His countenance was like lightning, and his clothing as white as snow. And the guards shook for fear of him, and became like dead men.

But the angel answered and said to the women, "Do not be afraid, for I know that you seek Jesus who was crucified. He is not here; for He is risen, as He said. Come, see the place where the Lord lay. And go quickly and tell His disciples that He is risen from the dead, and indeed He is going before you into Galilee; there you will see Him. Behold, I have told you."

So they went out quickly from the tomb with fear and great joy, and ran to bring His disciples word.

You will read that He had a choice. He didn't have to die. He could have called all His angels down and ended everything right then, but He didn't! Why? He loves you so much that He was willing to go through a great sacrifice to save you from your wrong choices that will separate you from Him for eternity.

Read John 3:13-18

No one has ascended to heaven but He who came down from heaven, that is, the Son of Man who is in heaven. And as Moses lifted up the serpent in the wilderness, even so must the Son of Man be lifted up, that whoever believes in Him should not perish but have eternal life. For God so loved the world that He gave His only begotten Son, that whoever believes in Him should not perish but have everlasting life. For God did not send His Son into the world to condemn the world, but that the world through Him might be saved. He who believes in Him is not condemned; but he who does not believe is condemned already, because he has not believed in the name of the only begotten Son of God.

Numbers 21:9

So Moses made a bronze serpent, and put it on a pole; and so it was, if a serpent had bitten anyone, when he looked at the bronze serpent, he lived. Just as the Israelites had to look at the bronze serpent to be saved from the deadly venom, we today need to look at the uplifted savior of the world, Jesus on a cross in order to be saved from our sins.

Is there anyone who would like to accept Jesus now? Let's Pray. Has everyone accepted Him? If not, do you know why? Can we talk about it?

> **Allow time for the youth to write honest feelings or beliefs. Go around and encourage each person to share. Pray for wisdom. This is not about judgement but to really help the group to see the life changing truth that our God is real, He is alive, and He really cares for each youth. He wants to be a part of the every day decisions they have to make and temptations that they face.**

Now that we have accepted Jesus and understand that He is the Word of God. What does living for Him mean? What do we do now?

Chapter 5

FINDING JESUS IN MY LIFE

Because of our past circumstances or situations, most of which are out of our control, we can have a clouded view of who we really are in Jesus. Taking time out to look at those areas will help us to see more clearly.

We also have hurts, shame, failures or hang-ups, that we carry with us every day. They effect the way we make decisions.

Let us look at what Jesus has to say about our short comings and our hurts that have been caused by others.

Read: Jeremiah 29:11-14

For I know the thoughts that I think toward you, says the Lord, thoughts of peace and not of evil, to give you a future and a hope. Then you will call upon Me, and go and pray to Me, and I will listen to you. And you will seek Me and find Me, when you search for Me with all your heart. I will be found by you, says the Lord, and I will bring you back from your captivity.

Do you have a hurt or concern that comes to mind today?

Have the youth write what comes to mind. They do not have to share out loud if they choose not to. The most important goal here is that they are honest and face the following questions.

Did you or do you have any control in the situation?

We are asking this to enlighten our youth about accountability. They might not have had any control in the situation and blame themselves. Leaders, pray for discernment. False guilt is hard. If they did have control, owning what they need to is essential to healthy thinking that leads to healthy actions in the future.

Did you or do you blame yourself?

Help them to place truth in what they are experiencing. Some will need more assurance and guidance. These questions will help you as a leader to see their 'heart' more clearly. You can witness more effectively when you can see them in a clearer light.

Why?

Help them to answer honestly! Freedom comes with truth. Point out errors that might hinder them from experiencing this freedom.

Did you ever resolve that matter?

If the matter is not resolved, the safety of our youth always comes first. If resolving it is a safe option, support him or her with courage to make the right decisions. Remember, it isn't always easy but it is right. If resolving the issue is not an option, pray and release it into the hands of Jesus.

What does resolving it look like to you?

Have the youth write down what seems right to him or her. If you are not sure, it is okay to let him or her know you will have an answer at a later time and validate the concern with confidentiality if needed. Encourage safe, healthy, truthful resolutions.

God wants to be involved in your everyday decisions, hurts and healing.

You can tell when you have allowed Jesus into your troubles because you will trust in Him while you go through the uncertainties. You will find a peace that will tell you it is going to be ok.

Read: John 14:27

Peace I leave with you, My peace I give to you; not as the world gives do I give to you. Let your heart not be troubled, neither let it be afraid.

Acts 4:12 "Nor is there salvation in any other, for there is no other name under heaven given among men by which we must be saved."

Prayer: First Jesus, I praise You and I thank You for coming to me. I need You and want You Jesus. I accept You into my heart. I want You to work in my circumstances. Please help me with this hurt. I lift it to You. I ask that You help me to forgive and that You turn my pain to Your glory as I trust in You. In Jesus name I pray. Amen.

Does a hurt come to mind that you caused on another person?

Give time for our youth to write. Let each youth know that it is important to write it down. This is their book and no one else has to see it, but truthfulness is the answer to freedom!

What was the situation?

Again, it is important for each teen to write about their actions. Actions have consequences. Whether our actions bless someone or cause someone harm, we do have an impact on others. The blessings come when make the right decision!

Do you know why you chose your decision?

Help each youth by really encouraging each one to be honest. If they are not able to be honest here, they will struggle with true relationships later in life. But, be sure to love them no matter what!

Did you ever resolve that matter?

If yes, how did it make them feel? If the answer is no, what are the issues that are holding them back. Encourage right behavior. Do the right thing. If it could be harmful, prayer is the bridge to bring them closer to resolution.

What does resolving it look like to you?

Be honest. Encourage the right action. It does not matter how the other person responds. It matters how we respond. We need to be God honoring!

When you learn just to talk to Jesus and trust that He hears you and is working the situation out for your good, you will see how good He is. You will learn how to trust Him in situations as they come. As you follow what Jesus shows you, you will feel whole and free to make good and right decisions. You will feel His love and forgiveness.

Lets see what Jesus has to say about pain that you have caused another.

Read: Psalms 103:1-5

Bless the Lord, O my soul; And all that is within me, bless His holy name! And forget not all His benefits: Who forgives all your wrongs, Who heals all your diseases, Who redeems your life from destruction, Who crowns you with loving kindness and tender mercies, Who satisfies your mouth with good things, So that your youth is renewed like the eagles.

Amen! Pray with them. They do not need to feel guilt. They need to experience Gods grace! Amen!

Chapter 6

FALLACIES TO LOOK OUT FOR

Remember a 'fallacy' is a false statement or deception.

Now we are going to look at a very personal issue. Schools are teaching it. The motto is something like, 'It's all good." The truth is, it's not all good. There are guidelines that God gave for us! They're for our good, so that a good life and not sorrowful emptiness in the end.

Leaders, it might be good to split up your group by gender during parts of this. Pray and be equipped for God to move. I pray His blessing and righteousness on you all.

> **God created man and woman. God created woman for man that he would not be alone.**

Read: Genesis 2:21-24

> *And the Lord caused a deep sleep to fall on Adam, and he slept; and He took one of his ribs, and closed up the flesh in its place. Then the rib which the Lord God had taken from man He made into a woman, and He brought her to the man.*

And Adam said:

"This is now bone of my bones

And flesh of my flesh;

She shall be called Woman,

Because she was taken out of Man."

Therefore a man shall leave his father and mother and be joined to his wife, and they shall become one flesh.

What does this mean to you?

Give the youth time to write. You might be surprised at some of their answers. Our youth have been taught by our schools, peers, or even parents very different views. Have grace. Truth is what we want to expose. Pray!

Lets look at the facts that supports Gods word. First, in forensic science, there are only two types of DNA. The DNA of a man and the DNA of a woman. There are no others. Second, Physically there are only two genders, a man and a woman. And third, medically, only two genders are proven. So we have forensic science, along with physical and medical evidence that confirms these facts.

The only stance, when a person claims to be something other than what they were born is their feelings.

What does this mean to you?

Give the teens time to write. Unfortunately, schools have placed this idea that we can be 'what ever gender' we want into our children. You will need to be patient in this area working through

the differences. **Remember, God loves each of us so much! We short change ourselves of His ultimate blessings when we chose a lifestyle that is in contradiction with His holy and righteous word.**

What does the Bible say about our feelings?

Give the teens time to talk about this and write. Let them share.
This gives us great insight into our young adults. We can better minister when we know where the true hearts of our youth are.

Read: Proverbs 28:26

He who trusts in his own heart is a fool, But whoever walks wisely will be delivered.

Remember, while we look at this, God loves everyone and sent His Son Jesus so that we might not perish. We all have a choice.

As I walk the halls of junior high and high schools, I see a lot of advertisement on just the very opposite of God's word. I see billboards and show cases that display books and information for you. It's wrong information. It is telling you young adults how to be homosexual, transgender, and what ever else they have chosen. They are saying that it is ok and normal behavior. Young adults, it is not ok.

You are in a very sensitive time of life. Your bodies are growing up. Your hormones are changing. This does not change God's best for you. See, the more you take God out of something, the worse it gets. Unbelievers have pushed God out of the schools and now they are pushing 'their' ideas in. You are the youth that will face this battle. This is where you will really need to look at truth and logic. Line it up to identify what is false.

In college, some are teaching that one in every ten people are born with both male and female parts. This is one of the biggest deceptions in school. Think about this. If one in every ten people were a different species, we would all know. It would be common.

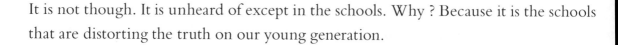

It is not though. It is unheard of except in the schools. Why ? Because it is the schools that are distorting the truth on our young generation.

Have you seen this around you? Explain.

Let each answer. Encourage honesty.

In the mean time, they are encouraging our youth by inviting them into false knowledge on how to change so they can become the opposite gender.

I personally know two young ladies that are beautiful people. I love them deeply. They both have fallen for this lie. Right now, one young lady's voice has changed. Not to sound like a man though, as she was told. It sounds very abnormal. She has turned very quiet and speechless. When she does speak, you see it in her eyes. She is starting to grow whiskers as well. Both these ladies give themselves shots everyday for this 'change'.

The other young lady keeps having allergic reactions and goes in and out of the hospital. Her voice is changing as well. But her voice just jumps around. This is not normal. This is abnormal. This is not nature. This is forced by what people want you to believe. These people are lost and have no value. They are ruining our young adults with no second thoughts. They ignore God and what He stands for, 'Right living'.

God still so loves these ladies. I do too. My heart goes out to them. I pray for them. What will happen to them in five or ten years? Only time will tell.

Take some time now and discuss what you have just read.

Teens, how does this make you feel? How do you view this and how does your view line up with the Bible?

Give each youth time to write and share. I am fairly confident that each individual knows someone in this category that they have established an friendship with. Encouraging truth with compassion is essential.

God created us to multiply and fill the earth.

What is multiply?

Group discussion. Always encourage the youth to write. Our thoughts now and our reflection later are essential when facing rough moments.

If you look at the body of a man and woman, they go together. They can reproduce and that's what the family unit is suppose to be.

Can two men reproduce? Can two women reproduce? Why?

Discuss the questions. Some might giggle with embarrassment. That is okay. We need to reach our youth with the truth as they are being taught fallacies all over the place.

Man was not made to be with another man and woman was not made to be with another woman. This is part of the compromising that we talked about in the beginning of this book.

Let us read what the Bible says in this matter.

Read: 1 Corinthians 6:9-11

> *Do you not know that the unrighteous will not inherit the kingdom of God? Do not be deceived. Neither fornicators, nor idolaters, nor adulterers, nor homosexuals, nor sodomites, nor thieves, nor covetous, nor drunkards, nor revilers, nor extortioners will inherit the kingdom of God. And such were some of you. But you were washed, but you were sanctified, but you were justified in the name of the Lord Jesus and by the Spirit of our God.*

This is not meant to scare you. It is to show you where God holds His Standard. Remember, He sent Jesus to wash our wrongs away. We just need to ask. He is telling us this so we know what is good for us and what is not. Remember, Jesus wants to be involved in our failures just as much as He wants to be in our successes!

What does this mean to you?

Share. Encourage. Validate. Pray.

How does this make you feel?

Be sensitive to some who will feel extremely hurt or disturbed by this chapter. Truth is truth. Truth does not compromise false ideas that will lead to destruction. Love and grace will help to show the love of Jesus when it is difficult. Stand in truth and love.

We are all sinners. We live in a world of people that make decisions everyday. Some directly impact our daily lives. The important thing is what we do when something happens.

Chapter 7

THE FINALE

As you learn to walk and grow in Jesus, remember that one of your strongest proofs is what the Bible says in Revelations 12:11.

Let's read it.

And they overcame him (satan) by the blood of the Lamb (Jesus crucifixion and resurrection) and by the word of their testimony.

What does that mean?

Write and share.

Your life will change. It will reveal Gods power in the transformation or the changing of your heart that takes place as you trust in Him! Others will see it and know that something great has happened to you! They will want to know what it is! Your testimony is what will give them the hope to experience the same thing they see you experiencing! Speak out to others about Gods miracles in your life and watch your faith grow stronger and stronger.

One of our hardest realizations is that most unbelievers, when they are asking questions, really want to know the truth! Do not hold back in fear. Fear is a tool that Satan will use to keep Gods living word from a heart that is seeking. Amen!

Do you have a testimony? Take a moment and write about it. May God's Riches and Peace be in your lives. Amen!

Have the youth capture their experience on paper. Remember, some may need your help.

Team up with a leader that you trust. Ask for him or her to help you while you learn to follow Jesus.

Let each one know that you are available for them and that they matter!

Let us pray and be there for you while you learn Gods peace and joy in everyday life.

No matter what!

Now the purpose of the commandment is love from a pure heart, from a good conscience, and from sincere faith....... 1 Timothy 1:5

* FIVE PROOFS:

1.) The universe is running down.

The universe is not eternal. Because it had a beginning, it will have an end.

The same goes for the earth. It's running down. It's like a light that you turn on and leave on. Eventually, the bulb does burn out.

2.) The universe is expanding.

(When God spoke the universe into existence, it was so powerful that it is still Expanding. AMAZING! Even though it will all come to an end, Gods power does not).

As scientists have discovered with COBE, they have found the universe is still growing.

3.) The radiation echo.

This was discovered in 1965. It was one of the most incredible discoveries of the last century. It's the cosmic background radiation. The afterglow from the initial explosion of light and heat that started at the moment creation began.

4.) Galaxy seeds.

Clusters of galaxies that form just right. If the continuous explosion of the universe expanding were going to fast, this would just collapse on itself. It's outburst movement is just right for these clusters to form.

5.) Albert Einsteins Theory.

Einstein discovered that there had to be a beginning. As he searched the universal question, this is what he had concluded. He didn't want his answer to be 'a beginning', he wanted to have concluded that it was 'always' there (the universe). He decided to add a zero to his discovery so that the answer would be as he wanted. As other physicist looked at it, they discovered his 'blunder'. He admitted to manipulating his findings, and that the logical conclusion was, the universe had to have a beginning.

If you wish to find out more, you can go online and investigate any of these proofs.

Bibliography

Josh McDowell *The* NEW EVIDENCE that demands a verdict, *Evidence I &II* copyright 1999 by Josh McDowell originally published by Here's Life Publishers, Inc. 1972, 1975, 1979, 1981 Campus Crusade for Christ, Inc.

I Don't Have Enough FAITH *to Be an* ATHEIST
Norman L. Geisler
Frank Turek
Published by Crossway 2004

The Encyclopedia of Biblical Prophecy
The Complete Guide to Scriptural Predictions and Their Fulfillment
1980
by Barton Payne

Special Thanks to my husband Christopher Burke who has been a wonderful support.

Printed in the United States
By Bookmasters